Wondrous Rhymes and Prayer Times

ARTWORK BY
The Land of Milk & Honey™

HARVEST HOUSE PUBLISHERS

EUGENE, OREGON

Wondrous Rhymes and Prayer Times

Text Copyright © 2005 by Harvest House Publishers
Eugene, Oregon 97402

ISBN-13: 978-0-7369-1542-7
ISBN-10: 0-7369-1542-7

The Land of Milk and Honey™ © 2005 by G Studios, LLC. The Land of Milk and Honey Trademarks owned by G Studios, LLC, Newport Beach, CA USA and used by Harvest House Publishers, Inc., under authorization. For more information regarding art prints featured in this book, please contact:

G Studios, LLC
4500 Campus Drive, Suite 200
Newport Beach, CA 92660
949.261.1300
www.gstudiosllc.com

Design and production by Garborg Design Works, Inc., Minneapolis, Minnesota

Harvest House Publishers has made every effort to trace the ownership of all poems and quotes. In the event of a question arising from the use of a poem or quote, we regret any error made and will be pleased to make the necessary correction in future editions of this book.

Scripture quotations are taken from the International Children's Bible, New Century Version, copyright © 1983, 1986, 1988 by Word Publishing, Dallas, Texas 75039. Used by permission.

Printed in China

05 06 07 08 09 10 11 12 / IM / 10 9 8 7 6 5 4 3 2 1

To

_____

With love,

_____

Sleep, my child, my darling, I sing to thee;

Silently the soft white moonbeams fall on thee and me...

COSSACK CRADLE SONG

Heavenly Father, hear my prayer;

Keep me in Thy loving care.

Guard me through the coming day,

In my work and in my play.

Keep me pure and strong and true,

Help me, Lord, Thy will to do.

Rock-a-bye, baby, thy cradle is green,
Father's a nobleman, mother's a queen.
And Betty's a lady, and wears a gold ring,
And Johnny's a drummer,
and drums for the king.

When I was down beside the sea
A wooden spade they gave to me
To dig the sandy shore.

My holes were empty like a cup,
In every hole the sea came up,
Till it could come no more.

ROBERT LOUIS STEVENSON

6

I had a little nut tree,
nothing would it bear

But a silver nutmeg,
and a golden pear.

The King of Spain's daughter
came to visit me,

And all was because of
my little nut tree.

I skipped over the water,
I danced over the sea,

And all the birds of the air,
they couldn't catch me.

MOTHER'S SONG

My heart is like a fountain true

That flows and flows with love to you.

As chirps the lark unto the tree

So chirps my pretty babe to me.

And it's O! sweet, sweet! and a lullaby.

There's not a rose where'er I seek,

As comely as my baby's cheek.

There's not a comb of honey-bee,

So full of sweets as babe to me.

And it's O! sweet, sweet! and a lullaby.

There's not a star that shines on high,

Is brighter than my baby's eye.

There's not a boat upon the sea,

Can dance as baby does to me.

And it's O! sweet, sweet! and a lullaby.

No silk was ever spun so fine

As is the hair of baby mine.

My baby smells more sweet to me

Than smells in spring the elder tree.

And it's O! sweet, sweet! and a lullaby.

A little fish swims in the well,

So in my heart does baby dwell.

A little flower blows on the tree,

My baby is the flower to me.

And it's O! sweet, sweet! and a lullaby.

The Queen has scepter, crown, and ball,

You are my scepter, crown, and all.

For all her robes of royal silk,

More fair your skin, as white as milk.

And it's O! sweet, sweet!

    and a lullaby.

Ten thousand parks

    where deer run,

Ten thousand roses in the sun,

Ten thousand pearls beneath the sea,

My baby more precious is to me.

And it's O! sweet, sweet! and a lullaby!

THE TREE IN THE WOOD

All in a wood there grew a fine tree,
The finest tree that ever you did see,
And the green grass grew around, around, around,
And the green grass grew around.

And on this tree there grew a fine bough,
The finest bough that ever you did see,
And the bough on the tree, and the tree in the wood,
And the green leaves flourished thereon, thereon, thereon,
And the green leaves flourished thereon.

Sing a song of sixpence,

A pocket full of rye,

Four and twenty blackbirds,

Baked in a pie.

When the pie was opened

The birds began to sing,

Was not this a dainty dish

To set before the king?

I see the moon, and the moon sees me,

God bless the moon, and God bless me!

THE LORD'S PRAYER

Our Father in heaven, we pray that your name
    will always be kept holy.
We pray that your kingdom will come,
We pray that what you want will be done,
    here on earth as it is in heaven.
Give us food we need for each day.
Forgive the sins we have done,
    just as we have forgiven those who did wrong to us.
Do not cause us to be tested;
    but save us from the Evil One.

A birdie with a yellow bill
Hopped upon the window sill,
Cocked his shining eye
and said:
"Ain't you 'shamed,
you sleepy head!"

ROBERT LOUIS STEVENSON

A SHIP A-SAILING

I saw a ship a-sailing,
A-sailing on the sea;
And oh! it was a-laden
With pretty things for me.

There were comfits in the cabin,
And apples in the hold;
The sails were made of satin,
The masts of beaten gold.

The four and twenty sailors
That stood between the decks,
Were four and twenty white mice,
With chains about their necks.

The captain was a duck, sir,
With a packet on his back,
And when the ship was sailing,
The captain said, "Quack! quack!"

NEW YEAR'S DAY

I saw three ships come sailing by,
Come sailing by, come sailing by;
I saw three ships come sailing by,
On New Year's day in the morning.

And what do you think was in them then,
Was in them then, was in them then?
And what do you think was in them then,
On New Year's day in the morning?

Three pretty girls were in them then,
Were in them then, were in them then.
Three pretty girls were in them then,
On New Year's day in the morning.

One could whistle, and one could sing,
The other could play on the violin,
Such joy there was at my wedding,
On New Year's day in the morning.

Of speckled eggs the birdie sings
And nests among the trees;
The tailor sings of ropes and things
In ships upon the seas.

The children sing in far Japan,
The children sing in Spain;
The organ with the organ man
Is singing in the rain.

ROBERT LOUIS STEVENSON

17

Sleep, baby, sleep!
Dad is not nigh,
Tossed on the deep,
Lul-lul-a-by!

Moon shining bright,
Dropping of dew,
Owls hoot all night,
To-whit! to-whoo!

Sleep, baby, sleep!
Dad is away,
Tossed on the deep,
Looking for day.

In the hedge-row
Glow-worms alight,
Rivulets flow,
All through the night.

Sleep, baby, sleep!
Dad is afar,
Tossed on the deep,
Watching a star.

Clock going—tick,
Tack—in the dark.
On the hearth—click!
Dies the last spark.

Sleep, baby, sleep!
What! not a wink!
Dad on the deep,
What will he think?

Baby dear, soon
Daddy will come,
Bringing red shoon
For baby at home.

All the World is full of things

God's true love and kindness brings;

In the air and on the ground,

In my home and all around,

God's great love is living.

O, how grateful I should be!

How my heart should try to see

Here and there and everywhere

All the thoughtfulness and care

God's great love is giving. Amen.

JOHN MARTIN

SCHOOL OVER

When our working school is done,
To the fields we go,
Walking in the grassy paths
Skipping we go.
Picking cooling buttercups,
Many pretty flowers,
Violets, forget-me-nots,
Spend happy hours.
Chase the bee and butterfly,
Where the summer daisies lie.
Ofttimes up the hills we go,
Gather pretty flowers,
Bluebells and daffodils,
Spending happy hours,
See little streamlets dance,
Down the hillside,
See the rocks the sunbeams glance,
Whence they glide.
Chase the bee and butterfly
Where the summer daisies lie.

How do you like to go up in a swing,
  Up in the air so blue?
Oh, I do think it the pleasantest thing
  Ever a child can do!

Up in the air and over the wall,
  Till I can see so wide,
Rivers and trees and cattle and all
  Over the countryside—

Till I look down on the garden green,
  Down on the roof so brown—
Up in the air I go flying again,
  Up in the air and down.

ROBERT LOUIS STEVENSON

Twinkle, twinkle, little star,
  How I wonder what you are,
  Up above the world so high,
  Like a diamond in the sky.
When the traveler in the dark
  Thanks you for thy tiny spark,
He could not see which way to go,
  If you did not twinkle so.
When the blazing sun is gone,
  And he nothing shines upon,
  Then appears thy tiny spark,
  Twinkle, twinkle, in the dark.

JANE AND ANNE TAYLOR

23

GIRLS AND BOYS COME OUT TO PLAY

Girls and boys come out to play,

The moon doth shine as bright as day;

Leave your supper and leave your sleep,

And come to your playfellows in the street.

Come with a whoop, come with a call,

Come with a good will or not at all.

Up the ladder and down the wall,

A penny loaf it will serve us all.

You find milk, and I'll find flour,

And we'll have a pudding in half an hour.

A CHILD'S PRAYER

Heavenly Father, hear my prayer!
Keep me always in your care!
Trying always to be good,
And to do the things I should;
Loving them that love me so,
And kind to every one I know.

J.T. TROWBRIDGE

24

Mistress Mary,

Quite contrary,

How does your garden grow?

With cockle shells

And silver bells,

And marigolds all in a row.

Sing hey diddle diddle,

The cat and the fiddle,

The cow jumped over the moon,

The little dog laughed

To see such craft,

And the dish ran away with the spoon.

Dear God, bless my Mother who
  Gives all her life and love to me
Her heart is tender, calm, and true,
  Her faith is boundless as the sea.
By wisdom that is brave and sure,
  By patience that is firm but mild,
She lives with but one object pure—
  To love and serve her little Child.

God, help me every day to prove
  How kind and loving I can be;
For surely all my Mother's love
  Should be reflected back from me.
O dear God, guide my growing Soul,
  So I may ever strive toward
Some noble purpose, higher goal,
  To make my life her best reward.

JOHN MARTIN

The friendly cow all red and white
I love with all my heart:
She gives me cream with all her might,
To eat with apple-tart.

She wanders lowing here and there,
And yet she cannot stray,
All in the pleasant open air,
The pleasant light of day.

And blown by all the winds that pass
And wet with all the showers,
She walks among the meadow grass
And eats the meadow flowers.

ROBERT LOUIS STEVENSON

Pat-a-cake! Pat-a-cake! Baker's man;
Pat it and bake it as fast as you can.
Prick it and prick it, and mark it with C,
And that will do purely for Charlie and me.

Little Jack Horner
Sat in a corner,
Eating his Christmas pie.
He put in his thumb,
And he pulled out a plum,
And said, What a good boy am I!

Little boy Blue,
    blow your horn,
The cow's in the meadow,
    the sheep in the corn.
But where is the little boy
    tending the sheep?
He's under the hayrick
    fast asleep.

The cuckoo is a pretty bird,
She sings as she flies,
She brings us good tidings,
And never tells lies.
She sucketh sweet flowers
To make her voice clear,
And when she sings cuckoo,
The summer draweth near.

A child should always say what's true
And speak when he is spoken to,
And behave mannerly at table;
At least as far as he is able.

ROBERT LOUIS STEVENSON

Wee Willie Winkie runs through the town,

Upstairs and downstairs in his night gown,

Tapping at the window, crying at the lock,

"Are the babes in their beds, for now it's ten o'clock?"

Tom shall have a new bonnet,

With ribbons so blue upon it.

With a hush-a-bye, and with a lull-a-bye,

And the moon is sailing all in the sky.

Old King Cole

Was a merry old soul,

And a merry old soul was he.

He called for his pipe,

And he called for his glass,

And he called for his fiddlers three.

Every fiddler, he had a fiddle,

And a very fine fiddle had he.

Twee-tweedle-dee, tweedle-dee,

   went the fiddlers.

Oh, there's none so rare

As can compare

With King Cole and his fiddlers three.

COUNTING SONG

One, two, buckle my shoe;

Three, four, shut the door;

Five, six, pick up sticks;

Seven, eight, lay them straight;

Nine, ten, a good fat hen;

Eleven, twelve, who will delve?

Thirteen, fourteen, draw the curtain;

Fifteen, sixteen, maids in the kitchen;

Seventeen, eighteen, who is waiting?

Nineteen, twenty, my stomach's empty,

Please, Mamma, give me some dinner.

Matthew, Mark, Luke, and John,

Bless the bed that I lie on,

Four corners to my bed,

Four angels round my head;

One to watch, and one to pray,

Two to bear my soul away.

The children live in heaven all day,
And if we watch them as they play
Perhaps we may some hint surprise
Of secret dealings with the skies.

They dance, they run, they leap, they shout,
They fling the torch of joy about:
Gay prodigals of golden mirth,
They lavish laughter on the earth.

Their fancy touches common things,
The very dust takes fairy wings:
The earth is all a box of toys
For lucky little girls and boys.

The children sleep in heaven all night,
Then meet the morning with delight,
And scamper out upon their way
To love and live in heaven all day.

M.A.
THE LIVING AGE, 1904

Children, you are very little,

And your bones are very brittle;

If you grow great and stately,

You must try to walk sedately.

You must still be bright and quiet,

And content with simple diet;

And remain, through all bewild'ring,

Innocent and honest children.

Happy hearts and happy faces,

Happy play in grassy places—

That was how, in ancient ages,

Children grew to kings and sages.

ROBERT LOUIS STEVENSON

Piping down the valley wild,
  Piping songs of merry glee,
On a cloud I saw a child,
  And he laughing said to me,

"Pipe a song about a lamb,"
  So I piped with merry cheer;
"Piper, pipe that song again,"
  So I piped—he wept to hear.

And I made a rural pen
  And I stained the water clear,
And I wrote my happy songs,
  Every child may joy to hear.

WILLIAM BLAKE

If you and I should join our hands
  And go at night soft through the hall,
I wonder could we hope to catch
  That shadow sliding from the wall?

He slips and slips and slips away,
  I touched his arm—and he was gone!
I cannot see his face, can you?
  What wall can that be painted on?

Because they say he isn't real,
  They say he's just a flattened form;
But me, I don't believe it's true,
  I touched his arm, and it was warm!

Right through the wall he slips and sinks:
  The room behind, you know is mine.
What can he want there in the dark?
  He never makes a sound or sign.

He never goes there in the day,
  Only at night, right after tea.
And then I go to bed, you know,
  And then he runs ahead of me.

If you will hold my hand quite close,
  And creep along with me quite still,
We'll make a sudden jump—but no!
  We'll touch him then—I know we will.

JOSEPHINE DODGE DASKAM

41

It is very nice to think

The world is full of

meat and drink,

With little children

saying grace

In every Christian

kind of place.

R OBERT   L OUIS   S TEVENSON

Sleep is a little man,

Sits on the stair,

Wears carpet slippers

And has white bushy hair.

Snores all night long,

As if it were a lark,

And then for his breakfast

He gobbles up the dark!

A DA   J ACK   C ARVER

God, please make me wise to see

   That Work is just as good as Fun,

Please help me to do it cheerfully,

   And purse to see it finely done.

When I have useful Work to do,

   Please make me very glad to do it;

And may I feel, dear God, that You

   Are always near to help me through it.

   While I am young, help me to see

      That I should work with might and main;

   For helpful Work is good for me,

      And strengthens body, heart, and brain.

      God, make me love my Work to-day,

      So I'll disdain to do it badly;

      And may I find some thoughtful way

      To work for others, well and gladly.

JOHN MARTIN

43

In winter I get up at night
And dress by yellow candle-light.
In summer, quite the other way,
I have to go to bed by day.

I have to go to bed and see
The birds still hopping on the tree,
Or hear the grown-up people's feet
Still going past me in the street.

And does it not seem hard to you,
When all the sky is clear and blue,
And I should like so much to play,
To have to go to bed by day?

ROBERT LOUIS STEVENSON

Dear God, to-day I moped around,
I almost sulked and acted blue;
I sighed and puttered, fussed and frowned,
And couldn't find a thing to do.

My eyes were blind, and didn't see
A hundred happy things, just meant,
To occupy a child like me,
And stop my selfish discontent.

O God, please help my heart to find
The happy things that come each day.
Please give just the sort of mind
That thinks in just the wisest way.

O help me every day I live
To see the blessings You have sent.
But, best of all, dear God, please give
My heart the blessing of content. Amen.

JOHN MARTIN

45

What are little boys made of, made of

What are little boys made of?

Snaps and snails, and puppy-dogs' tails;

And that's what little boys are made of, made of.

What are little girls made of, made of,

What are little girls made of?

Sugar and spice, and things that are nice;

And that's what little girls are made of, made of.

God made the sun

And God made the tree,

God made the mountain

And God made me.

I thank You, O God,

For the sun and the tree,

For making the mountains,

And for making me.

LEAH GALE

48